To Sibani

Love o best Wishes

From Sheila

THE CREATIVE COOK

Mouthwatering

MEDITERRANEAN

LEWIS ESSON

FOREWORD BY VALENTINA HARRIS

PHOTOGRAPHY BY JULIE FISHER

St Michael

In memory of Colin Clark who taught me how
useful it was to 'have spaghetti up your sleeve'

Please note the following:

Quantities given in all the recipes serve 4 people unless otherwise stated.

Spoon measurements are level unless otherwise stated.

Metric and imperial measures are both given, use one or the other as the two are not interchangeable.

Flour used is plain white flour, unless otherwise specified.

Preparation of ingredients, such as the cleaning, trimming and peeling of vegetables and fruit, is presumed and the text only refers to any aspect of this if unusual, such as onions used unpeeled etc.

Citrus fruit is generally coated in a layer of preservative wax. For this reason, whenever a recipe uses the rind of oranges, lemons or limes the text specifies unwaxed fruit. If organic uncoated fruit is not available, scrub the fruit vigorously in hot soapy water, rinse well and pat dry.

Eggs used are size 3 (65 g/2¼ oz) unless otherwise specified. The Government recommends that eggs not be consumed raw, and people most at risk, such as children, old people, invalids and pregnant women, should not eat them lightly cooked. This book includes recipes with raw and lightly cooked eggs, which should not be eaten by the above categories. These recipes are marked by a * in the text. Once prepared, these dishes should be kept refrigerated and used promptly.

Editorial Direction: Lewis Esson Publishing
Art Director: Mary Evans
Design: Peter Butler
Illustrations: Alison Barratt
Food for Photography: Meg Jansz
Styling: Jackie Boase
Editorial Assistant: Penny David
Production: Julia Golding

First published in 1992 for Marks and Spencer plc by Conran Octopus Limited,
37 Shelton Street, London WC2H 9HN

British Library Cataloguing in Publication Data
A catalogue record for this book is available from the British Library

ISBN 1-85029-432-1

Typeset by Hunters Armley Ltd
Printed and bound by Arnoldo Mondadori Editore, Verona

CONTENTS

FOREWORD

As I write this, the rain is dripping miserably out of a dull grey English sky. It is supposed to be summer here, but the air is as chilled, damp and cold as it is in mid-November. Homesickness for the warm embrace of my homeland sweeps through me. I long to be strolling round a noisy Sicilian street market, where the sunlight bounces off the brilliant reds, yellows, greens and purples of the piles of glorious juicy produce; where the smells of freshly brewed espresso and baking bread and brioches comes wafting out of every cafe doorway that I pass.

I'd like to join in with the early preparation of the vineyards for the summer heat. And when I'm hot and sweaty from the morning's toil, (because spring in Sicily is completely different from the wintry scene in my Norfolk garden!), I'd like to sit under a cool pergola, where I would settle down to the important business of feeding my body, but most especially my soul, with a plate of pasta dressed with a fragrantly scented, deliciously rich sauce, and then savour the fishermen's morning catch which has just come off the wonderfully chaotic, brightly painted wooden smacks. This would be accompanied by mounds of vegetables grown to an incredible size and level of perfection on the nearby volcanic slopes of Etna. Then crusty bread drizzled with deep-green olive oil (just to wipe my plate quite clean) and fresh ewes' milk cheeses, and huge perfumed fruit . . .

Perhaps it would be more constructive to prepare my own feast, right here and now. A trip to the local supermarket cannot quite replace the passion and fervour of the midday pitch in a Sicilian street market, but the variety of flavours, colours and textures and the sheer availability have improved immeasurably over the last few years. I am delighted to be able to fill my English kitchen with the scent of fresh basil, to drizzle olive oil over the garlic-rubbed slices of ciabatta bread, to slice into a mozzarella that is freshly made today – with the secure knowledge that there is plenty more where that came from, just nearby!

Books like *Mouthwatering Mediterranean* help to banish these cold days and bring to life the riches of the food treasures of my homeland. In the summer – provided the weather permits you to indulge in *al fresco* eating – this wonderful and comprehensive book will help you to create a complete Mediterranean feast. The recipes contained in this book are not specifically Italian or Spanish or Greek. They simply celebrate the joy and warmth of the Mediterranean and allow you to bask in its many seductive pleasures. I am delighted that the ingredients and the recipes are at last so readily accessible that the magic of the region can weave a spell on you, so that in the time it takes to boil the pasta it can transport you to the sights, scents and sounds of the *Mouthwatering Mediterranean* . . .

VALENTINA HARRIS

SOUPS, STARTERS AND MEZZE

*I*n many Mediterranean countries a wide variety of small snacks and titbits is an important part of the culinary tradition, like *tapas* in Spain and *mezze* in Greece, Turkey and the Middle-east. As simple as a bowl of olives or a dip, or as complex as vine leaves or filo pastries filled with all manner of stuffings, they are served all through the day in cafés and bars. A common practice is to start a meal with a selection of such dishes, and to follow this with a plainly cooked piece of fish or meat – or even just a salad. Sometimes an entire meal is composed of such dishes. The abundance of good vegetables grown in the region has also

made substantial soups a common meal in themselves, often topped with a thick highly flavoured sauce and served with good local crusty bread.

Clockwise from the left: Pissaladière (page 10), Crostini with Wild Mushrooms (page 11) and Bruschette with Tomatoes (page 10)

PISSALADIÈRE

FOR THE DOUGH

½ sachet (5.5 g/1½ tsp) active dried yeast
250 g/8½ oz flour, plus more for dusting
1 egg, lightly beaten
½ tsp salt
1 tbsp olive oil

FOR THE TOPPING

5 tbsp olive oil
1 k/2¼ lb onions, very thinly sliced
3 garlic cloves, crushed
bay leaf
1 tsp chopped fresh thyme or ½ tsp dried thyme
1 tsp chopped fresh basil or ½ tsp dried basil
1 tsp chopped fresh rosemary or ½ tsp dried rosemary
3 tbsp red wine
1 tbsp capers, drained and mashed
225 g/8 oz canned chopped plum tomatoes, drained
24 canned anchovy fillets, drained and cut in half
lengthwise
24 small black stoned olives
salt and freshly ground black pepper

PISSALADIERÈS, a speciality of the Provence region of France, are flat open tarts not dissimilar to Italian pizzas.

First make the dough: dissolve the yeast in 5 tablespoonfuls of warm water. Sift the flour into a warm bowl and form a well in the centre of it.

When the yeast mixture is spongy, pour it into the middle of the well together with the egg and salt. Gradually mix in the flour from the edges until the mixture forms a smooth dough.

Turn it out on a floured surface and knead for 5 minutes until smooth and elastic.

Generously grease a bowl with the oil, place the ball of dough in it and turn the ball well to coat it thoroughly with the oil. Cover with a damp cloth and leave in a warm place to rise for 1 hour, or until it has risen to about twice its original size.

Meanwhile make the topping: put 4 tablespoons of oil in a large frying pan (preferably with a lid) over a moderate heat and add the onions, garlic, bay leaf and other herbs. Season well and cook gently for about 5 minutes until the onions are translucent. Add the wine, capers and tomatoes. Stir well, cover and cook very gently for about 30 minutes more, until the onions are very soft.

Preheat the oven to 250C/475F/gas9 and grease a 25.5 cm/10 in pie or pizza pan, or a baking sheet, with a little of the remaining olive oil.

Remove the risen dough from the bowl and knead it briefly on a lightly floured surface to knock it back slightly and incorporate the oil. Then roll it out and use it to line the pie or pizza dish or simply press it into the dish so that it is higher at the edges and there is a hollow in the centre. Alternatively, form the dough into such a round container on the prepared baking sheet.

Adjust the seasoning of the onion mixture and spoon it into the centre of the pie, leaving a broad rim round the edge. Using the strips of anchovy, make a lattice pattern on top of the filling and press the olives into the spaces between. Brush the uncovered rim with the remaining olive oil and leave the pissaladière in a warm place for about 15 minutes to rise a little more.

Bake for 20–25 minutes, until the dough is crisp and brown, and serve hot or warm.

NOTE: defrosted frozen bread dough, pizza dough or shortcrust pastry works very well in this recipe.

BRUSCHETTE WITH TOMATOES

2 ciabatta loaves
2 large garlic cloves, crushed
4 tbsp extra virgin olive oil
4 large very ripe tomatoes, halved
salt and freshly ground black pepper
tiny basil or tarragon leaves, to garnish (optional)

Preheat a hot grill.

Split each loaf across in half lengthwise (start by cutting the crusts with a knife, but try to prise the halves apart and not to slice all through cleanly, as it is necessary to create a rough surface on which to rub the tomatoes). Then cut each of these pieces in half.

Grill the pieces of bread, rough sides uppermost, until they are just beginning to brown around the top edges.

While the bread is still very warm, spread each piece with some crushed garlic, brush generously with oil and then smear a tomato half all over its surface to spread the tomato pulp on it. Season well.

Return to the grill briefly just to warm through for serving and then garnish with the leaves, if using.

BRESAOLA WITH LEMON MUSTARD VINAIGRETTE

2 unwaxed lemons
5 tbsp extra virgin olive oil
2 tsp English mustard
20 slices of bresaola
2 tbsp finely chopped flat-leaf parsley
salt and freshly ground black pepper
about 12 tiny cherry tomatoes, to garnish
radicchio leaves, to garnish

Finely grate 2 teaspoons of zest from one of the lemons and extract 1 tablespoon of its juice. Cut the other lemon into wedges.

In a small bowl, blend the lemon zest and juice with the oil, mustard and seasoning to taste.

Fan the slices of beef out decoratively on a plate. Just before serving, mix the dressing together well again and dribble it over the slices of beef.

Sprinkle with the parsley, garnish with the cherry tomatoes nestling in radicchio leaves and serve with the lemon wedges.

CROSTINI WITH WILD MUSHROOMS

4 tbsp extra virgin olive oil
4 garlic cloves, finely chopped
255 g/9 oz mixed sliced wild mushrooms, preferably including some ceps
3 tbsp lemon juice
2 tbsp chopped flat-leaf parsley
8 thick slices of crusty white bread
3 tsp anchovy paste
1 buffalo Mozzarella cheese, thinly sliced
salt and freshly ground black pepper
cayenne pepper

Preheat a hot grill or the oven to 180C/350F/gas4.

In a large frying pan, heat 2 tablespoons of the oil over a moderate heat and sauté the garlic gently until translucent. Add the mushroom slices and sauté over a moderate to high heat until the mushrooms are just beginning to give off their liquid.

Increase the heat and cook briskly for a few minutes until the liquid is driven off and the mushrooms are beginning to brown. Stir in the lemon juice, together with most of the parsley. Season.

Meanwhile lightly grill the slices of bread, or bake them, until they are just beginning to brown.

Spread the toasted slices of bread sparingly with the anchovy paste and then brush them with the remaining oil. Spoon the sautéed mushroom mixture in heaps in the centres of them, reserving some of the better-looking mushroom slices for garnish.

Cover the mushrooms with slices of Mozzarella and sprinkle some pepper over the cheese. Grill or bake in the oven until the cheese is bubbling.

Garnish with the reserved mushrooms and parsley and dust lightly with cayenne before serving piping hot.

Bresaola is a speciality of Italy's Lombardy province. Best quality beef is sliced very thinly and air-cured.

Bruschette may be described as Italian garlic bread while crostini are more like a type of toasted sandwich, although in Italy both are mostly cooked in the oven.

If wild mushrooms are difficult to obtain for the Crostini, use equal parts button mushrooms, oyster mushrooms, or brown caps and dried ceps (porcini), soaked in warm water for 20 minutes.

MINESTRONE VERDE WITH PESTO

SERVES 8

55 g/2 oz dried haricot beans, soaked overnight
5 garlic cloves, crushed
piece of salted pork rind or 2 slices of fatty bacon, diced
3 tbsp olive oil
2 small leeks, thinly sliced
2 celery stalks, with their leaves, chopped
3 tbsp chopped flat-leaf parsley
1 tbsp chopped basil
225 g/8 oz fine French beans, cut into 2.5 cm/1 in pieces
55 g/2 oz shelled peas
2 small courgettes, cut into thick julienne strips about
2.5 cm/1 in long
1 small cabbage, shredded
1 large potato, finely diced
225 g/8 oz canned chopped plum tomatoes
85 g/3 oz vermicelli
2 tbsp chopped chives
freshly grated Parmesan cheese, to serve

FOR THE PESTO
55 g/2 oz fresh basil leaves
2 garlic cloves
45 g/1½ oz pine kernels
45 g/1½ oz grated Parmesan cheese
3 tbsp extra virgin olive oil

Rinse the haricot beans and simmer them in unsalted boiling water with 2 of the garlic cloves and the pork rind or bacon for about 2 hours or until the beans are just beginning to become tender. Drain and discard the garlic and pork rind or bacon.

In a large heavy-based pan, heat the oil over a gentle heat. Add the leeks, remaining garlic, the celery, half the parsley and the basil. Season generously and cook gently until all the ingredients are softened but not browned.

Add 1.1 litre/2 pt of warm water together with

the haricots and remaining vegetables including the tomatoes with their liquor. Bring to the boil and simmer gently until all the vegetables are tender.

Meanwhile make the pesto: pound the basil leaves with the garlic and pine kernels in a mortar with a pestle. Add the cheese a little at a time until the mixture is a thick paste. Then mix in the oil a little at a time, making sure it is entirely incorporated before adding any more. The finished sauce should have the consistency of creamed butter.

A few minutes before serving, crush the vermicelli into small pieces and add these to the soup. When these are just tender, stir in the remaining herbs and warm through gently.

Serve with a little pesto swirled on top of each serving and pass the Parmesan separately.

AVGOLEMONO*

1.1 litre/2 pt good chicken or vegetable stock
3 garlic cloves
115 g/4 oz long-grain rice
3 eggs
(*see page 2 for advice on eggs)
juice of 2 large lemons
salt and freshly ground black pepper
2 very thin lemon slices, halved, to garnish
4 tbsp chopped flat-leaf parsley, to garnish

Bring the stock to the boil and add the garlic cloves and the rice. Simmer for about 15 minutes, until the rice is just tender. Remove and discard the garlic.

Just before serving, beat the eggs lightly and then beat in some of the lemon juice until the mixture is pale and foaming. Stir a ladleful of the hot stock into the egg mixture, beating continuously. Then return the mixture to the stock, again stirring constantly. Almost immediately remove the stock from the heat: the soup must not boil. or the eggs will curdle.

Adjust the seasoning with salt and pepper and add just enough of the remaining lemon juice to give the soup a good sharp taste. Garnish with the lemon slices and chopped parsley to serve.

AVGOLEMONO *is a classic Greek soup, flavoured with eggs and lemons. When the egg and lemon juice mixture is added the soup thickens to a rich creamy texture. The delicate flavour depends on using a good stock and on careful seasoning.*

SPICY HUMMUS WITH TAHINI

Now familiar all over the world, the Middle-eastern chickpea purée Hummus traditionally appears on most mezze tables. Such purées may simply be flavoured with garlic and salt, or – as here – with lemon juice, cumin and tahini paste, made from crushed sesame seeds, to give a fine nutty flavour. The earthy taste of tahini is also essential to the classic Turkish aubergine dip Baba Ghanouj. The aubergines must also first be charred to impart the right degree of smokiness. Serve both these dips with strips of pitta bread or crudités, such as celery stalks, sticks of cucumber and courgette, and sweet pepper strips.

250g/8 oz dried chickpeas, soaked overnight, or 450 g/1 lb canned cooked chickpeas, drained
3 or 4 large garlic cloves, crushed
juice of 3 lemons
3 tbsp extra virgin olive oil
2 tsp ground cumin
150 ml/¼ pt tahini paste
2 tbsp finely chopped flat-leaf parsley
salt
cayenne pepper
1 tbsp toasted pine kernels, to garnish (optional)
pitta bread, cut into strips, to serve

Rinse the chickpeas thoroughly (carefully removing any debris and shed skins). Cover the chickpeas with water, bring to the boil and simmer them until quite tender: just over 1 hour for dried chickpeas and only 10-15 minutes for canned chickpeas.

Drain thoroughly, reserving a little of the liquid, and put the chickpeas into a food processor or mash them in a bowl. Add the garlic, lemon juice, 2 or 3 tablespoons of the cooking liquid, 1 tablespoon of oil, 1 teaspoon of cumin, a generous pinch of salt and a pinch of cayenne.

Add most of the tahini paste and mix again to a good thick creamy consistency. Adjust the consistency, if necessary, with more tahini paste or cooking liquid or lemon juice. Adjust the seasoning with more salt and cayenne.

Turn the mixture out into a shallow soup bowl. Mix the remaining oil with a pinch of the cayenne and a pinch of the remaining cumin. Dribble this over the top of the hummus.

Sprinkle with the parsley and decorate with the remaining cumin and some more cayenne (a star pattern is traditional). Dot with the pine kernels, if using. Serve with pitta strips or crudités.

BABA GHANOUJ

2-3 large aubergines
3 large garlic cloves, crushed
1 small onion, grated
pinch of paprika
juice of 2 large lemons
100 ml/3½ fl oz tahini paste
salt
2 tsp finely chopped mint, coriander or flat-leaf parsley, to garnish
tiny stoned black olives, to garnish
1 tbsp olive oil, to serve
pitta bread or crudités, to serve

Preheat a fairly hot grill or the oven to 230C/450F/gas8.

Either grill the aubergines, turning them regularly, or bake them in the oven for about 30 minutes, until the skins are black and blistered.

Allow them to cool slightly and then peel off the charred skin. Wash the aubergines and squeeze them firmly to extract their bitter juices.

Chop the aubergine flesh coarsely and put into a blender or mash it in a bowl. Add the garlic, onion, a large pinch of salt, paprika and some of the lemon juice. Blend lightly and then add alternating small amounts of the tahini paste and remaining lemon juice. The final consistency should be thick and smooth. Adjust this and the seasoning with more salt, tahini or lemon juice.

Turn out into a serving bowl and garnish with the herbs and olives. Just before serving with pitta bread or crudités, dribble the oil over the top.

Clockwise from the top left: Assorted Filo Pastry Parcels (page 16), Vine Leaves Stuffed with Seafood Mousse (page 17), Baba Ghanouj, baby aubergines, black olives and Spicy Hummus with Tahini served with crudités

VEGETABLES, SALADS AND EGG DISHES

*M*ore than anything else, it is the extraordinary range of fresh vegetables – brought to perfect ripeness by weeks of glorious sunshine – which forms the basis of Mediterranean cooking. Their brilliant colours and full rich flavours are used to advantage in the many vegetable dishes, such as *ratatouille* and *caponata*, traditional all over the region. The abundant fresh herbs also contribute their freshness and aromatic subtlety, especially to salads. Eggs and cheeses, such as Parmesan, Ricotta, Mozzarella, Feta and goats' cheese, are also often teamed with vegetables in baked dishes or salads to great effect.

Clockwise from the right: Courgette Gratin (page 20), Grilled Vegetables with Lemon Dressing (page 21), Red Peppers Stuffed with Fennel (page 20) and more grilled vegetables

Sicilian Caponata, like its close French relation ratatouille, is served cold as an hors d'oeuvre or warm as a vegetable dish in the summer, traditionally piled into a dome shape on the plate.

Tabbouleh, a salad of bulghar wheat and herbs, originated in the mountains of Lebanon. The freshness of the parsley and mint perfectly balance the pungency of the raw onion and garlic to produce a dish that is uniquely refreshing. Coriander leaves are also often included.

CAPONATA

2 aubergines, cut into 1 cm/½ in cubes
16 canned anchovies, drained
about 3 tbsp olive oil
1 large onion, sliced
2 garlic cloves, finely chopped
225 g/8 oz canned chopped plum tomatoes, drained
bouquet garni
2 tbsp tomato paste
3 tbsp sherry vinegar or white wine vinegar
2 large courgettes, cut into large dice
1 large red sweet pepper, deseeded and diced
1 large green sweet pepper, deseeded and diced
55 g/2 oz capers, with a little of their liquid
2 or 3 stalks of celery, thinly sliced
85 g/3 oz stoned black olives, cut into strips
2 tbsp finely chopped flat-leaf parsley
salt and freshly ground black pepper

Put the aubergine pieces in a colander, sprinkle well with salt and leave to drain for about 15 minutes. Rinse well and pat dry. Rinse the anchovies in warm water, pat dry and cut into strips.

Preheat the oven to 180C/350F/gas4 and grease a large ovenproof casserole with a little of the oil.

Heat the remaining oil in a large pan and cook the onion gently for 2 or 3 minutes until soft. Add the garlic and cook for a minute or so more.

Stir in the tomatoes, bouquet garni and tomato paste. Simmer for about 20 minutes, until reduced to a thick purée. Discard the bouquet garni. Stir in the vinegar and simmer for 1 more minute.

Mix the aubergines, courgettes and peppers into the tomato purée together with the anchovies, capers, celery and olives. Adjust the seasoning.

Spoon into the casserole, cover and bake for about 1½ hours, or until all the vegetables are quite tender.

Serve warm or cool, sprinkled with the finely chopped parsley.

TABBOULEH

170 g/6 oz bulghar wheat
6 tbsp olive oil
juice of 3 lemons
2 garlic cloves, very finely chopped
3 onions, finely chopped
small bunch of fresh mint
250 g/8 oz ripe juicy tomatoes, finely chopped
½ cucumber, finely diced
large bunch of flat-leaf parsley, finely chopped
salt and freshly ground black pepper
2 or 3 small spring onions, chopped, to garnish
tiny mint leaves, to garnish
small cos lettuce leaves, to serve

Put the bulghar in a large bowl and cover well with warm water. Leave for about 20 minutes to swell and soften. Drain thoroughly, squeezing to remove excess moisture, and place in a large serving bowl.

Mix the olive oil, two-thirds of the lemon juice, the garlic and onions. Season to taste and pour this dressing over the bulghar. Stir well and leave for at least 20 minutes more.

Just before serving, finely chop the mint, reserving a few of the best small leaves for garnish. Mix the chopped mint into the salad, together with most of the tomatoes, the cucumber and parsley. Adjust the seasoning with more salt, pepper and lemon juice, as necessary (it should taste quite sharp).

Garnish with the remaining chopped tomatoes, the chopped spring onions and the reserved whole mint leaves. Serve with small cos lettuce leaves to act as scoops.

Left: Tabbouleh; right: Provençal Vegetables with Goats' Cheese (page 24)

SALADE NIÇOISE

225 g/8 oz tiny French beans
225 g/8 oz ripe tomatoes, cut into wedges
1 green sweet pepper, deseeded and cut into strips
1 cucumber, cut into thick strips
55 g/2 oz canned anchovies, drained
55 g/2 oz stoned black olives
200 g/7 oz canned tuna fish in oil, drained and flaked
4 hard-boiled eggs, shelled and quartered
5 tbsp olive oil
1 tbsp white wine vinegar
1 garlic clove, crushed
2 tbsp chopped flat-leaf parsley
salt and freshly ground black pepper

In its native South of France, SALADE NIÇOISE commonly also contains broad beans and artichokes. In Britain, lettuce and cooked potatoes are popular additions.

Blanch the beans briefly until just tender and refresh in cold running water. Pat dry.

Mix the vegetables in a large salad bowl (or arrange in separate piles around the bowl). Arrange the anchovies, olives, flaked tuna and eggs over the top.

Make a dressing by vigorously mixing the oil, vinegar and garlic with seasoning. Pour this over the salad and sprinkle with the parsley.

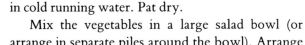

PROVENÇAL VEGETABLES WITH GOATS' CHEESE

1 small round goats' cheese, weighing about 75 g/2½ oz (see below)
115 g/4 oz broccoli florets
115 g/4 oz fine French beans
115 g/4 oz mange-tout peas
2 small courgettes, cut into thick sticks
2 large garlic cloves
4 tbsp olive oil
1 tbsp lemon juice
pinch of dried thyme
4 or 5 ripe juicy tomatoes, coarsely chopped
2 spring onions, finely chopped
salt and freshly ground black pepper
pine kernels or strips of marinated red sweet pepper, to garnish (optional)

Select a cheese which is firm but not too dry.

In a large pan of boiling salted water, blanch the vegetables in batches until just tender but still very firm to the bite: about 6 or 7 minutes for the broccoli, 5 minutes for the beans, and 2 or 3 minutes for the peas and courgettes.

Drain each batch of vegetables promptly as they are ready and refresh them under cold running water. Drain well, pat dry and leave to cool.

Make the dressing: put the cheese, garlic, oil, lemon juice and thyme in a blender. Mix until smooth.

Add the tomatoes in small batches, processing each until smooth. Add just enough to give the dressing a rich consistency which is thick but sufficiently runny to coat the vegetables. Season well.

Put the cooled vegetables in a large bowl and pour over the dressing. Toss well to coat all the ingredients thoroughly. Scatter over the spring onions and garnish with pine kernels or strips of marinated pepper, if using.

SWEET PEPPER SALAD

1 large red sweet pepper
1 large green sweet pepper
1 large yellow sweet pepper
18 stoned black olives
3 tbsp olive oil
juice of 1 large lemon
3 garlic cloves, crushed
3 tbsp finely chopped flat-leaf parsley
salt and freshly ground black pepper

Preheat a hot grill. Halve the peppers and remove their seeds and pith.

Grill the pepper halves, skin-side upwards, until the skins are black and blistering.

Allow to cool a little and then skin them. Cut the flesh into strips and mix in a salad bowl or on a serving plate.

Finely chop half the olives and halve the others.

Make the dressing by mixing the oil, lemon juice, chopped olives, garlic and half the parsley. Season well with salt and pepper.

Dribble the dressing over the peppers and toss well. Sprinkle the salad with the remaining parsley and dot with the olive halves to serve, either still quite warm or cold.

For a very filling main-course salad, add about 140 g/5 oz lean bacon which has been cut into strips and dry-fried until crisp.

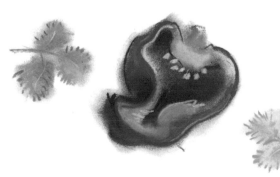
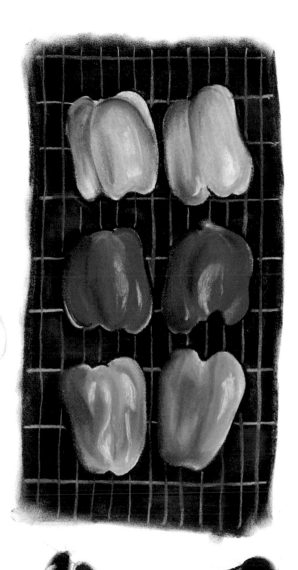

MOZZARELLA AND TOMATO SALAD WITH AVOCADO

2 buffalo Mozzarella cheeses, thinly sliced
2 beef tomatoes, thinly sliced
small basil leaves, to garnish
FOR THE AVOCADO DRESSING
1 large ripe avocado
1 tbsp balsamic vinegar
1 large red onion, finely chopped
4 tbsp olive oil
salt and freshly ground black pepper

First make the dressing: halve and stone the avocado and scoop the flesh out into a bowl. Add the vinegar and mash the onion into the avocado flesh.

Gradually add the oil, mixing all the time, until it has all been incorporated. Season to taste.

On a flat serving plate, arrange the Mozzarella and tomato slices in alternating rows. Either dribble the dressing over the centres of the rows or have it in a pool in the centre of the serving plate. Garnish with the basil leaves.

SCRAMBLED EGGS WITH SWEET PEPPERS*

85 g/3 oz butter
1 tbsp oil
1 green sweet pepper, deseeded and cut into julienne strips
1 red sweet pepper, deseeded and cut into julienne strips
2 garlic cloves, finely chopped
pinch of thyme
2 tbsp balsamic vinegar
8 large eggs
*(*see page 2 for advice on eggs)*
1 or 2 dashes of Worcestershire sauce
salt and freshly ground black pepper
chopped chives, to serve

Traditional tasty Mozzarella cheeses made from buffaloes' milk are now available from many good food stores and delicatessens.

In a large heavy-based frying pan, melt one-third of the butter with the oil over a low to moderate heat. Add the pepper strips, garlic and thyme. Season and cook gently 2 or 3 minutes. Tip into a bowl and pour over the vinegar. Cover and keep warm.

Melt the remaining butter in the pan. Lightly beat the eggs with some seasoning and Worcestershire sauce. Pour into the pan and cook very gently, stirring all the time until just becoming thick.

Serve immediately on warmed plates. Stir the pepper mixture and spoon some over the eggs. Sprinkle with chives to serve.

NOTE: this dish may also be served on toast, or in hollowed-out baked bread croûtes, or even in blanched sweet pepper halves.

SWISS CHARD AND PINE KERNEL TART

30 g/1 oz butter
1 tbsp olive oil
1 onion, finely chopped
2 large garlic cloves, finely chopped
285 g/10 oz Swiss chard leaves
6 tbsp finely chopped flat-leaf parsley
juice of ½ lemon
250 g/8½ oz frozen shortcrust pastry, defrosted
2 eggs, beaten
45 g/1½ oz pine kernels
150 ml/¼ pt crème fraîche
6 tbsp milk
pinch of freshly grated nutmeg
salt and freshly ground black pepper
flour, for dusting
sun-dried tomatoes in oil, to garnish (optional)

Preheat the oven to 180C/350F/gas4.

Melt the butter in the oil in a large sauté pan over a moderate heat. Sauté the onion and garlic until translucent and then add the Swiss chard, parsley, lemon juice and some seasoning.

Sauté briefly over a fairly high heat until the chard is softened. Set aside.

Roll the pastry out on a lightly floured surface and use it to line a 25.5 cm/10 in tart pan. Cover the base with foil or baking paper and weight with beans.

Bake blind for about 10 minutes and then remove the weights and paper. Return to the oven for another 10 minutes or so, until the pastry is firm but not yet brown. Brush with a little of the beaten egg and return to the oven for 5 minutes.

While the tart case is baking, toast all but 1 tablespoon of the pine kernels on a baking sheet for 5-10 minutes, until just a good golden brown.

In a bowl, mix the cream, milk, eggs and nutmeg. Season and stir in the chard mixture. At the last minute; stir in the toasted pine kernels.

Pour into the pastry case, scatter over the remaining pine kernels and bake for 20 minutes.

Garnish with chopped sun-dried tomatoes in oil, if wished.

NOTES: spinach may be used instead of the Swiss chard. Some chopped bacon or ham may be cooked with the chard for extra flavour.

Alternatively, for a delicious and unusual sweet tart, replace the onions, garlic, parsley and seasoning with sultanas and honey and a pinch of allspice.

TORTILLLAS, *or Spanish omelettes, are a mainstay of the traditional selections of snacks served in tapas bars. They are served warm or cold, cut into thick wedges or squares.*

SALSA *is the Spanish and Italian word for sauce, but it is now commonly used in English for dressings spiced with chilli.*

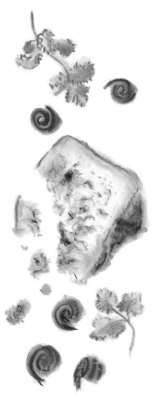

COURGETTE TORTILLA WITH A HERB SALSA

SERVES 4–6

2 large potatoes, diced small
30 g/1 oz butter
2 tbsp olive oil
2 onions, finely chopped
3 garlic cloves, finely chopped
3 large courgettes, thinly sliced
8 eggs, beaten
2 tbsp chopped flat-leaf parsley
salt and freshly ground black pepper
FOR THE HERB SALSA
5 tbsp olive oil
1 tbsp red wine vinegar
1 tsp grainy mustard
5 tbsp canned chopped plum tomatoes, drained
pinch of chilli powder
2 tbsp each chopped chives and flat-leaf parsley

In a large pan of boiling salted water, blanch the potato dice for 2 or 3 minutes. Refresh under cold running water, drain well and pat dry.

In a 25.5 cm/10 in frying or omelette pan, preferably with a lid, melt the butter with the oil over a moderate heat.

Sauté the onion and garlic until the onion is translucent and soft. Add the courgettes and potatoes and sauté for a few minutes more, taking care that the onion and garlic do not get too brown.

Season the eggs and stir in most of the parsley. Stir into the pan, cover and cook over a gentle heat for about 10 minutes, until the eggs are just set.

Meanwhile, preheat a hot grill. Finish the omelette off under it until the top is well browned.

While the tortilla is cooking, make the salsa by mixing all the ingredients and seasoning to taste.

Serve the tortilla warm or cold, sprinkled with the remaining parsley. Serve the salsa separately.

GORGONZOLA AND ANCHOVY SOUFFLÉ

55 g/2 oz unsalted butter
55 g/2 oz canned anchovy fillets, drained
1 level tbsp flour
150 ml/¼ pt milk
3 eggs, separated
85 g/3 oz Gorgonzola cheese, crumbled or cubed
freshly ground black pepper
cayenne pepper

Preheat the oven to 190C/375F/gas5 and heat a baking sheet in the centre of it. Carefully grease a 15 cm/6 in soufflé dish with 15 g/½ oz of the butter. Make sure that the rim is well greased to prevent the soufflé catching as it rises.

Rinse the anchovies to remove excess saltiness, pat them dry and cut them into small strips.

In a large heavy-based pan, melt two-thirds of the remaining butter over a low heat and stir in the flour. Cook for a minute or two, stirring continuously. Gradually add the milk, still stirring, and cook until smooth and thick.

Off the heat, stir the egg yolks into the sauce, one at a time. Then stir in the cheese and anchovies. Adjust the seasoning with pepper and cayenne pepper (the seasoning should be quite forceful as it will be cut by the unseasoned egg white). Set aside.

Whisk the egg whites to stiff peaks. Spoon a little of the beaten egg white into the cheese mixture and stir well to 'slacken' the mixture. Carefully fold the remaining egg white into the mixture.

Pour the mixture into the prepared soufflé dish. Tap the base fairly hard on a work surface and place in the oven on the hot baking sheet.

Bake for 20–25 minutes, until well-risen and golden. Serve immediately, dusted with cayenne.

Courgette Tortilla with a Herb Salsa

FISH, MEAT AND POULTRY

*T*he emphasis on vegetables and grains, together with the practice of composing meals of many small dishes, means that meat and poultry do not hold the same dominant position in Mediterranean kitchens as they do in ours. They are generally reserved for the high days and holidays, or seen much more as flavouring ingredients and used in wonderful combinations with rice, pasta and vegetables, as in *moussaka* or kebabs. On the other hand, the Mediterranean peoples have always made much of the abundance of fish and seafood readily available to them, especially the nutritious and health-giving oily fish, such as mackerel, sardines and tuna, served plainly grilled, stuffed with herbs or blended into rich purées.

Top: Bouillabaisse with Rouille (page 32); Bottom: Baked Red Mullet with Rosemary (page 33)

Conger eel, gurnard
and the
Mediterranean
rascasse, or scorpion
fish, are essential for
an authentic version
of the Provençal fish
soup
BOUILLABAISSE,
but any good
selection of white and
firm-fleshed fish will
do. The soup must
boil vigorously as
this emulsifies the oil.

The spicy
mayonnaise
ROUILLE is a
popular
accompaniment to
many fish dishes,
especially soups.
Traditionally, slices
of bread are spread
with a little rouille,
placed in the bottom
of deep bowls and the
broth poured over.

BOUILLABAISSE WITH ROUILLE*

SERVES 6–8

*1 k/2¼ lb mixed whole white fish, such as whiting, bass,
haddock, cod, red mullet, monkfish and red snapper*
*675 g/1½ lb whole rich fish, such as striped bass, mackerel
and eel*
225 g/8 oz mussels
3 onions
3 leeks
3 celery stalks
2 pinches of saffron
450 g/1 lb canned chopped plum tomatoes
4 garlic cloves, crushed
bouquet garni
½ small fennel bulb, finely chopped
thin strip of orange rind
bunch of flat-leaf parsley
175 ml/6 fl oz olive oil
bay leaf
juice of ½ lemon
1 tbsp tomato paste
salt and freshly ground black pepper
thick slices of country bread, toasted, to serve

FOR THE ROUILLE

4 garlic cloves, chopped
2 egg yolks
(*see page 2 for advice on eggs)
1 tsp cayenne pepper
6 tbsp olive oil
1 or 2 tbsp tomato paste

Buy the fish whole but make sure that the
fishmonger has scaled them thoroughly. Cut all the
fish into large chunks, reserving the heads and tails.
Place the pieces in a large bowl, keeping the white
and rich fishes separate. Scrub the mussel shells well,
discarding any which do not close on being tapped.

Cut one each of the onions, leeks and celery stalks
into large pieces and chop the rest of them.

Soak the saffron in a few spoonfuls of warm
water and add half of it to the bowl of fish along with
the chopped onions, leeks and celery, the tomatoes,
garlic, bouquet garni, fennel, orange rind and
two-thirds of the parsley, finely chopped. Pour over
the oil and season well. Cover and leave to marinate
for an hour or two in a cool place.

Meanwhile, place all the fish trimmings in a large
pan. Add the vegetables which have been cut into
large pieces, most of the remaining bunch of parsley,
the bay leaf and lemon juice and just cover
with water. Season and bring to a simmer. Simmer
for 20 minutes and then strain through a sieve.

Remove the pieces of fish from the marinade and
set aside. Tip the remaining contents of the bowl into
a large saucepan. Add the strained fish stock and the
remaining saffron and its water. Bring to the boil and
simmer for about 30 minutes.

While this cooks, make the rouille: put the garlic
and eggs in a food processor along with cayenne and
a tiny pinch of salt. Blend to a thick paste and, with
the machine still running, add the oil in a thin steady
stream as if making mayonnaise. The sauce should
have a thick creamy consistency. Colour it with
tomato paste and season with more salt and cayenne
as necessary (it should be quite spicy).

Bring the simmering liquid to a rapid boil and add
the chunks of rich fish and the prepared mussels.
Continue to boil as rapidly as possible for about 6
minutes and then add the white fish chunks.
Continue to cook in the same way for another 5
minutes, or until the flesh of the white fish flakes
readily. Transfer the fish and shellfish to a warmed
serving dish, discarding any mussels which have
failed to open. Remove the bouquet garni and
orange rind from the broth and pour it into a
warmed tureen. Add just enough tomato paste to
give a good colour and adjust its seasoning. Snip the
remaining parsley over fish and the broth to garnish.

BAKED RED MULLET WITH ROSEMARY

4 tbsp olive oil
85 g/3 oz shallots, finely chopped
2 garlic cloves, crushed
6 sprigs of rosemary
250 ml/8 fl oz dry white wine
4 small red mullet, scaled and gutted, but with their livers retained
juice of 1 lemon
2 tbsp finely chopped flat-leaf parsley
salt and freshly ground black pepper
lemon wedges, to serve

Preheat the oven to 230C/450F/gas8 and grease a baking dish with some of the oil.

Put the shallots and garlic in a saucepan with 2 rosemary sprigs, cut in half. Add all but 6 tablespoons of the wine and boil until reduced by about three-quarters, to leave the softened shallots and a sticky liquid. Discard the rosemary.

With a sharp knife, make some shallow cuts into the back of the fish to allow the heat to permeate. Slip a rosemary sprig and some seasoning into the cavity of each fish.

Spread the shallot mixture in the bottom of the baking dish, season and arrange the fish on top, alternating heads and tails. Dribble over the remaining oil and wine and bake for 15 minutes, basting from time to time.

Sprinkle with the lemon juice and parsley to serve, accompanied by lemon wedges.

MARINATED SARDINES

8 fresh sardines, cleaned and filleted
300 ml/½ pt olive oil
1 large onion, thinly sliced
3 garlic cloves, finely chopped
strip of unwaxed orange rind
2 or 3 sprigs of thyme
2 or 3 sprigs of rosemary
bay leaf
juice of 2 lemons
salt and freshly ground black pepper
cayenne pepper
2 tbsp finely chopped flat-leaf parsley, to garnish
lemon wedges, to serve

Put the sardine fillets in a large sauté pan and add half the oil. Heat to a gentle simmer and cook until golden. Turn and cook the other sides in the same way. Transfer the sardines to a deep dish.

Mix the onion, garlic, orange rind, herbs and lemon juice into the oil in the pan together with the remaining oil and 3 tablespoons of water. Season with salt, pepper and a large pinch of cayenne.

Bring to the boil and simmer for about 15 minutes. Leave to cool slightly, then pour the cooled mixture over the sardines and leave to marinate overnight.

To serve, sprinkle with the chopped parsley and garnish with lemon wedges.

Serve the MARINATED SARDINES *with crusty bread and a green salad.*

BACCALÀ IN GOLDEN BREAD CROÛTES

450 g/1 lb salt cod
4 thick slices from a square white loaf
45 g/1½ oz butter, melted
200 ml/7 fl oz olive oil
2 garlic cloves
about 150 ml/¼ pt single cream, warmed
2 tsp walnut oil
1 tbsp lemon juice
pinch of nutmeg
salt and freshly ground black pepper
1 tbsp finely chopped flat-leaf parsley, to garnish
lemon wedges, to serve

BACCALÀ, or salt cod, is popular in the cooking of many Mediterranean countries, from Spain and Portugal to Greece. The French have their own celebrated version of the fish, puréed with oil and milk, known as brandade de morue. Thorough soaking of the fish to remove excess saltiness is essential.

Soak the salt cod for 1 or 2 days, ideally under cold running water, to remove excess saltiness.

Drain the fish and put it in a large pan with cold water to cover. Cover, bring to the boil and simmer very gently for 6 or 7 minutes, until just tender.

Drain and leave to cool until it can be safely handled. Remove and discard all skin and bones and flake the flesh into a large bowl.

Preheat the oven to 180C/350F/gas4.

Trim out a deep hollow on one side of each slice of bread, taking care not to tear all the way through. Using a pastry brush, paint the pieces of hollowed-out bread all over with melted butter.

Bake the croûtes for 15-20 minutes, or until a good uniform golden colour. Remove from the oven and, while still warm, carefully rub them all over with one of the garlic cloves. Keep warm.

While the croûtes are baking, warm 150 ml/¼ pt of the oil in a heavy-based pan. When very hot, reduce the heat and add the fish. Using a wooden spoon, beat in the fish over a very gentle heat.

When the mixture begins to be really mushy, crush in the remaining garlic and stir it in. Transfer to a large mortar or food processor. Start adding the

remaining oil and the warmed cream in alternating small amounts, pounding or blending in each addition thoroughly before adding any more. Be careful not to over-process or the mixture will lose its texture.

The resulting purée should be smooth and stiff enough to hold a shape. Stir in the walnut oil, lemon juice and nutmeg and season to taste.

Spoon the mixture into and around the croûtes and sprinkle with the parsley to serve, accompanied by lemon wedges and a tomato salad.

GRILLED SOLE WITH LEMON AND PARMESAN

2 unwaxed lemons
8 Dover sole fillets, skinned
45 g/1½ oz butter, melted
3 tbsp grated Parmesan cheese
salt and freshly ground black pepper
lemon wedges, to serve

Finely grate 1 tablespoon of zest from 1 of the lemons and extract the juice from them both.

Rinse the sole fillets, pat them dry and lay them in a shallow baking dish. Mix the lemon zest into the juice and season with a little salt and some pepper. Pour this over the fish and leave to marinate for about 30 minutes, turning the fillets from time to time.

Preheat a moderate grill.

Remove the fish from the marinade. Arrange the fillets in the grill pan and brush the tops with some butter. Grill for 5-7 minutes, until just done. Then turn the fillets, brush the other sides with butter and sprinkle with the Parmesan. Grill for another 5-7 minutes until the cheese is melted and golden.

Serve the sole immediately with the pan juices poured over them and with lemon wedges.

NEAPOLITAN STEAKS WITH PIZZAIOLA SAUCE

4 thick rump or sirloin steaks
2 tbsp olive oil
salt and freshly ground black pepper
FOR THE PIZZAIOLA SAUCE
2 tbsp olive oil
2 onions, finely chopped
4 garlic cloves, finely chopped
1 small red pepper, deseeded and finely chopped
675 g/1½ lb very ripe tomatoes, chopped
large pinch of oregano
3 tbsp coarsely chopped flat-leaf parsley
dash of Tabasco sauce

First make the sauce: heat the oil in a saucepan and sauté the onions for 2 or 3 minutes, until lightly coloured. Add the garlic and chopped red pepper and cook for a minute or so more.

Add the tomatoes, oregano and most of the parsley. Season with salt and pepper and Tabasco. Cover and simmer gently for about 15 minutes, stirring from time to time. The tomatoes should not be allowed to become too pulpy.

Towards the end of this time, over a fairly high heat put the oil in a large sauté pan which has a lid. Season the steaks and brown them rapidly on both sides.

Once the steaks are browned on both sides, reduce the heat to very low and pour the sauce over them. Cover and cook for 3-7 minutes, depending on how well done the steaks are to be. Adjust the seasoning, if necessary.

Serve the steaks with their cooking sauce poured over them and sprinkled with the reserved parsley.

NOTE: try adding some chopped mushrooms to the sauce for extra flavour.

FRUIT AND NUT KOFTA

1 k/2¼ lb minced lean steak or lamb, or a mixture
30 g/1 oz butter
2 onions, finely chopped
2 garlic cloves, crushed
55 g/2 oz pine kernels
3 or 4 dried apricots, finely chopped
55 g/2 oz seedless raisins
2 eggs, lightly beaten
pinch of allspice
2 tbsp flour
2 tbsp grated Parmesan cheese
2 tbsp olive oil
salt and freshly ground black pepper
chopped flat-leaf parsley, to garnish
lemon slices, to serve

Ask the butcher to pass the meat through the mincer 2 or 3 times to get the right consistency.

Melt the butter in a large sauté pan over a moderate heat and sauté the onion, garlic and pine kernels briefly until just beginning to colour.

Transfer these to a large bowl and knead together with the meat, fruit, eggs, allspice and salt and pepper. Form into walnut-sized meatballs.

In a shallow plate, mix the flour and cheese and season well. Roll the meatballs in the mixture.

Add the oil to the pan and sauté the meatballs quite gently until golden brown and cooked right through.

Arrange in concentric circles on a warmed serving plate, garnish with parsley and serve with lemon slices.

These meatballs are delicious served hot with a lemony yogurt or spicy tomato sauce and accompanied by rice or potatoes. They are equally good cold with salad or as part of a buffet or picnic.

A classic of Neapolitan cuisine, PIZZAIOLA is a rich and highly flavoured tomato sauce used with meat and pasta.

KOFTA, or meatballs, are ubiquitous in Arab cooking, although they vary widely from place to place in their exact ingredients. They may even be shaped into fingers or flat cakes, like hamburgers. For the right melting texture the meat must be minced at least two or three times, or pulsed in a food processor until smooth.

YOGURT MOUSSAKA

SERVES 6–8

2 aubergines, thinly sliced
about 100 ml/3½ fl oz olive oil
350 g/12 oz lean minced steak or lamb
4 large onions, thinly sliced
3 large garlic cloves, finely chopped
3 tbsp finely chopped flat-leaf parsley
400 g/14 oz canned chopped plum tomatoes, drained
5 tbsp tomato paste
2 eggs
450 ml/¾ pt Greek yogurt
2 tbsp lemon juice
pinch of freshly grated nutmeg
55 g/2 oz Parmesan cheese
salt and freshly ground black pepper

The Greeks claim
MOUSSAKA as their
own dish, although
the Turks adopted it
and spread it
throughout the
Islamic world. This
version uses yogurt
and eggs instead of
the more usual white
sauce.

Put the aubergine slices in a colander and sprinkle them generously with salt. Leave to drain for about 30 minutes and then rinse thoroughly. Pat dry.

Heat 2 tablespoons of the oil in a large frying pan over a moderate heat and brown the aubergine slices in batches, draining them on paper towels as they are ready and adding more oil to the pan as needed.

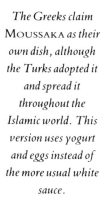

Add 1 or 2 more tablespoons of the oil to the pan, increase the heat to high and brown the meat by spreading it out into a flat cake and cooking this rapidly, undisturbed, until the underside is well coloured. Then break up the cake, stir the meat well and form it into a flat cake yet again. Cook in the same way. Repeat this process until the meat is a good uniform colour. Transfer to a bowl.

Heat 1 or 2 more tablespoons of the oil in the pan over a moderate heat and cook the onions for 2 or 3 minutes until soft. Add the garlic and parsley and cook for a minute or so more. Add the tomatoes, browned meat and tomato paste and simmer for about 30 minutes. Season well.

Preheat the oven to 180C/350F/gas 4 and grease a deep baking dish generously with 1 tablespoon of the remaining oil.

Put a layer of one-third of the aubergine slices in the bottom of the prepared dish. Spoon over half the meat mixture and then repeat the layers, finishing with a layer of aubergine slices.

Mix the eggs into the yogurt and season with salt, pepper, lemon juice and nutmeg. Pour this over the contents of the dish. Sprinkle Parmesan over the top and bake for about 45 minutes, until golden brown.

NOTE: try adding layers of sautéed mushrooms or courgettes, par-boiled potatoes or spinach, or slices of Gruyère cheese for extra interest. (You can then even omit the meat to make a vegetarian moussaka.) Add some red wine or 1 or 2 spoonfuls of brandy to the onions for extra flavour.

HONEYED LAMB KEBABS

1.35 k/2 lb boned leg of lamb, cut into 2.5 cm/1 in cubes
4 onions, cut into quarters
4 tomatoes, quartered
2 red sweet peppers, quartered and deseeded
2 green sweet peppers, quartered and deseeded
8 bay leaves
chopped oregano or flat-leaf parsley, to garnish
lemon wedges, to serve
FOR THE HONEY MARINADE
1 unwaxed lemon
4 tbsp honey
6 tbsp olive oil
2 garlic cloves, crushed
2 tbsp chopped oregano
2 tsp crushed black peppercorns

First make the honey marinade: finely grate 1 teaspoon of lemon zest and extract the lemon juice. Mix these with the remaining ingredients in a bowl. Add the pieces of lamb and onion quarters and stir well to coat them thoroughly. Cover and leave in a cool place for a few hours, stirring occasionally.

Preheat a hot grill or barbecue. Drain the pieces of lamb and onion well and thread them on skewers interleaved with pieces of tomato, pepper and bay leaves.

Grill until well browned on all sides, basting with the marinade from time to time.

Garnish with chopped oregano and serve with lemon wedges and accompanied by a green, mixed or tomato and onion salad.

NOTE: add rolled bacon slices or quartered mushrooms to the kebabs for extra interest. Try replacing the oregano with mint, rosemary or basil.

Clockwise from the top: Fruit and Nut Kofta (page 35) with a lemon-yogurt sauce, Honeyed Lamb Kebabs with a spicy tomato sauce, and Chicken Drumsticks with Garlic and Lime (page 39)

MOROCCAN LEMON CHICKEN

4 unwaxed lemons
1 large corn-fed or free-range chicken, dressed weight about
1.5 k/3½ lb, but giblets retained
2 onions
bay leaf
1 tsp black peppercorns
3 tbsp finely chopped flat-leaf parsley
1 tbsp olive oil
1 tsp finely chopped fresh root ginger
pinch of cinnamon
3 tbsp finely chopped coriander leaves
salt and freshly ground black pepper

Preheat the oven to 220C/425F/gas7.

Grate 1 tablespoon of zest from the lemons and pare off 2 or 3 thin strips of rind. Quarter 2 of the other lemons.

Trim the giblets, removing any gall taint and put in a small pan with 1 of the onions, the bay leaf, peppercorns, the strips of lemon rind and any stalks from the parsley. Cover with water, bring to the boil and simmer gently for about 1 hour. Strain.

Finely chop the remaining onion. Heat the oil in a sauté pan over a moderate heat and sauté it briefly, together with the grated lemon zest, ginger, cinnamon and seasonings, until the onion is soft.

Transfer to a bowl and mix in most of the herbs. Stuff the chicken with this mixture and the lemon quarters, squashing them lightly as you insert them.

Place the chicken in a roasting pan, breast downwards. Add just enough water to cover the base and cook for about 50-60 minutes, turning over half-way through and basting regularly, until well browned all over and the juices run clear when the thickest part of the thigh is pierced.

Transfer the chicken to a warmed serving plate, tipping it so that any liquid inside the bird drains back into the pan. Garnish with one of the remaining lemons, cut into wedges and the remaining herbs.

Deglaze the roasting pan with the juice from the last of the lemons, scraping up any sediment with a wooden spoon, and boil briefly to reduce to a sticky liquid. Add the giblet stock and boil to reduce to a sauce-like consistency. Adjust the seasoning and serve this sauce separately, adding any juices that run from the chicken during carving.

In North Africa this dish would be made using lemons which have been dried or preserved in oil, giving a much more pungent flavour.

The ancient Persian
FAISINJAN *sauce of*
pomegranates and
walnuts was used
mostly for wild duck
and other game birds,
but suits chicken and
domesticated duck. If
fresh pomegranates
are unavailable, use
2 or 3 tablespoons of
pomegranate syrup
made up with
300 ml/½ pt of
water instead of the
sieved juice, but do
not add sugar.

RABBIT WITH PRUNES, OLIVES AND BACON

1 large dressed rabbit, cut into pieces
115 g/4 oz stoned prunes, halved
2 tbsp oil
1 tbsp flour
300 ml/½ pt red wine
300 ml/½ pt chicken stock
2 garlic cloves, finely chopped
bouquet garni
140 g/5 oz streaky bacon, rinded and cut into strips
85 g/3 oz stoned black olives, halved
salt and freshly ground black pepper
FOR THE MARINADE
300 ml/½ pt red wine
2 tbsp oil
1 large onion, coarsely chopped
1 large carrot, coarsely chopped
12 peppercorns
bay leaf

Mix the marinade ingredients in a bowl and add the rabbit and prunes. Stir well, cover and leave in a cool place for 2-3 hours or overnight, stirring occasionally.

Using a slotted spoon, remove the rabbit, prunes and vegetables from the marinade and pat dry.

Heat the oil in a large flameproof casserole over a moderate heat and brown the rabbit pieces in it.

Remove the rabbit and brown the vegetables. Sprinkle over the flour and sauté for a minute or so.

Stir in the marinade, wine and stock together with the garlic, bouquet garni and seasoning. Return the rabbit pieces to the casserole. Bring to the boil, cover and simmer gently for about 30 minutes.

Towards the end of this time, dry-fry the bacon until browned. Add this, the olives and prunes to the casserole and cook for a further 15 minutes.

Transfer rabbit and vegetables to a serving dish. Boil the juices rapidly to reduce them to a sauce.

DUCK BREAST FAISINJAN

4 pomegranates
juice of 1 large lemon
1 tbsp brown sugar or honey
4 boned duck breasts or 2 large French magrets
1 tbsp olive oil
1 onion, finely chopped
85 g/3 oz walnuts, chopped
salt and freshly ground black pepper

Halve the pomegranates and scoop the seeds out into a food processor, reserving 2 or 3 tablespoons. Blend briefly and then press through a sieve.

Put the juice obtained into a saucepan and add half its volume of water, the lemon juice, sugar and seasoning. Bring to the boil and simmer gently for about 20 minutes. Allow to cool.

Prepare the duck breasts by scoring the fat with diagonal cuts down to the flesh along its length.

Put the duck breasts in a bowl and pour over the cooled pomegranate mixture. Stir well, cover and leave to marinate for 2 or 3 hours.

Preheat a hot grill. Drain the duck breasts, reserving the marinade. Pat them dry and grill fat side up for 5-8 minutes, until well browned. Turn and cook the other side in the same way. (Duck is best served fairly pink; if you prefer it well done, reduce the heat and cook for another 10 minutes or so.)

While the duck is cooking, heat the oil in a saucepan over a moderate heat and add the onion and walnuts. Cook gently for 2 or 3 minutes until the onion is soft. Add the pomegranate mixture to the saucepan, bring to the boil and simmer for about 5 minutes. Adjust the seasoning and the sweet-and-sour balance with more lemon juice or sugar.

Serve the duck thickly sliced, sprinkled with the reserved seeds and with the sauce served separately.

Duck Breast Faisinjan garnished with watercress

RICE, GRAINS AND PASTA

Perhaps the peak of creativity in Mediterranean cooking is reached in their cunning ways of using staples like rice and grains. Scarcely ever served as mere plain accompaniments, they are cooked slowly with flavouring ingredients to make dishes as splendid as *risotto, paella,* and *lasagne.* Less common grains such as couscous, polenta and bulghar wheat are also cooked with rich sauces or made into refreshing salads. The versatility of pasta has been most people's first glimpse of this amazing inventiveness. The myriad different pasta shapes available can be combined with literally innumerable sauces to make anything from light snacks to substantial meals – and even interesting desserts.

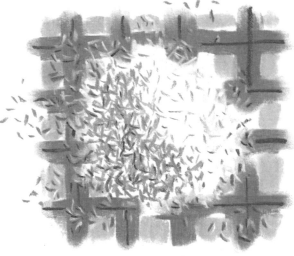

Saffron Paella (page 46) with an array of rice, pasta, pulses and flavouring ingredients.

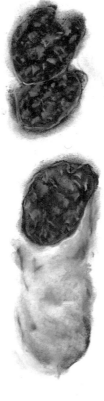

There are endless variations on the Spanish rice dish PAELLA – only rice, oil and saffron are essential. Other ingredients may include green beans, shelled peas and artichoke hearts, lobster, duck and rabbit.

SAFFRON PAELLA

SERVES 6–8

1 chicken, dressed weight about 1.35 k/3 lb, cut into 12 pieces, backbone and giblets retained
4 onions
3 large garlic cloves, chopped
white of 1 leek, chopped
1 celery stalk, thinly sliced
bouquet garni
12 black peppercorns
350 g/12 oz squid, sliced into rings
about 18 mussels
4 tbsp olive oil
250 g/9 oz chorizo sausage, sliced
1 large red sweet pepper, deseeded and cut into thick strips
1 large green sweet pepper, deseeded and cut into thick strips
few strands of saffron
6 large tomatoes, peeled and chopped
350 g/12 oz long-grain rice
6-8 langoustines or Dublin Bay prawns (optional)
salt and freshly ground black pepper
cayenne pepper
lemon wedges, to serve

Put the chicken giblets and backbone in a pan with 2 of the onions coarsely chopped, the garlic, leek, celery, bouquet garni, peppercorns and a large pinch of salt. Barely cover with water and bring to the boil. Skim and then simmer for about 1 hour.

Meanwhile, put the squid in a pan and cover with cold water. Bring to the boil and simmer for 5 minutes, drain and set aside. Scrub the mussel shells well, discarding any open ones which do not close when tapped. Finely chop the remaining onions.

Heat the oil in a large deep frying or paella pan over a moderate heat and brown the chicken pieces. Remove them with a slotted spoon and set aside.

In the same oil, cook the chorizo, squid, pepper strips and chopped onions gently for a few minutes. Stir in the saffron and cook for another 5 minutes. Add the tomatoes, and bring to the boil. Season well and add a good pinch or two of cayenne.

Stir in the rice. Place the chicken pieces, mussels and langoustines, if using, on top. Pour over the strained chicken stock and bring to the boil.

Cover and simmer gently for about 20 minutes, or until the rice is tender. Keep checking the rice; if it looks too dry at any time, add a little water. Serve with lemon wedges.

SALAMI AND BLUE CHEESE RISOTTO

45 g/1½ oz butter
2 tbsp olive oil
1 large onion, finely chopped
2 large garlic cloves, finely chopped
350 g/12 oz risotto rice, preferably arborio
850 ml/1½ pt hot chicken or veal stock
225 g/8 oz Italian salami, peeled and cubed
225 g/8 oz Gorgonzola or other blue cheese
2 celery stalks, chopped
1 large red pepper, deseeded and cut into thin strips
large pinch of dried sage
2 tbsp finely chopped flat-leaf parsley
salt and freshly ground black pepper
cayenne pepper
chopped chives, to garnish

In a large heavy-based pan which has a tight-fitting lid, melt the butter with the oil over a moderate heat. Add the onion and garlic. Cook gently for 1 or 2 minutes until soft and just beginning to colour.

Add the rice and sauté over a fairly high heat for 2 minutes. Add 300 ml/½ pt of stock, stir well and bring to the boil. Reduce the heat and simmer gently for about 5 minutes, until the stock is absorbed.

Continue to add the remaining stock, one-quarter at a time, stirring well and waiting until it has all been absorbed before adding more. The whole process should take about 30 minutes and the final result should be rice which is richly creamy and slightly sticky – but not mushy.

About half-way through, add half the salami and cheese with the celery, red pepper and sage.

With the final addition of stock, add the remainder of the salami and cheese and the parsley. Adjust the seasoning with salt, pepper and cayenne. Serve garnished with the chives.

CHICKEN AND LAMB COUSCOUS

SERVES 6–8

2 tbsp oil
1 large chicken, cut into 12 pieces, backbone retained
250 g/8½ oz lean stewing lamb, cut into large cubes
3 onions, chopped
4 garlic cloves, crushed
3 turnips, cut into chunks
3 large carrots, chopped
few strands of saffron
½ tsp each of ground cumin, ginger and turmeric
4 large ripe tomatoes, chopped
4 courgettes, chopped
85 g/3 oz seedless raisins
bunch of flat-leaf parsley, finely chopped
bunch of coriander, finely chopped
200 g/7 oz canned cooked chickpeas, drained
450 g/1 lb pre-cooked couscous
2 tsp harissa paste
30 g/1 oz butter
2 or 3 tbsp rose water
55 g/2 oz stoned dates, cut into shards
salt and freshly ground black pepper
more harissa paste, to serve

In the bottom part of a couscoussier or a large heavy-based saucepan, heat the oil over a fairly high heat and brown the pieces of chicken and lamb.

Add the onions, garlic, turnips, carrots and the chicken backbone. Cover with water, season and stir in the saffron and other spices. Bring to the boil and simmer for about 1 hour, skimming as necessary.

Remove and discard the backbone. Add the tomatoes, courgettes, raisins, most of the herbs and two-thirds of the chickpeas. Simmer for 30 minutes more.

Either prepare the couscous by simply pouring boiling water over it, leaving it to steep for about 10 minutes and draining it, or by steaming it for about 20 minutes in the top part of the couscoussier.

Ladle out 2 cupfuls of the broth and season it with a little of the harissa. When the couscous is fluffed up and ready, stir in one-third of this seasoned broth along with the butter, the remaining chickpeas, rose water and dates.

Serve the couscous on a large warmed serving dish with the pieces of meat and vegetables piled in the centre and some of the broth poured over. Sprinkle with the reserved herbs and serve the remaining seasoned broth and more harissa separately.

LENTIL AND BULGHAR PILAF WITH YOGURT

225 g/8 oz green lentils, preferably le Puy
bay leaf
1 tsp cumin seeds, finely crushed
1 tsp coriander seeds, finely crushed
225 g/8 oz bulghar wheat
pinch of cayenne
6 tbsp olive oil
2 onions, thinly sliced
2 garlic cloves, finely chopped
2 tbsp finely chopped coriander leaves
juice of ½ lemon
150 ml/¼ pt Greek yogurt
salt and freshly ground black pepper

Soak the lentils in cold water for about 1 hour, drain and put them in a pan. Pour in 1.1 litre/2 pt of fresh water and add the bay leaf and spices. Bring to the boil and simmer for about 20 minutes until just tender.

Remove the bay leaf and add the bulghar wheat with a pinch of cayenne and seasoning to taste. Stir well, cover and turn off the heat. Leave to sit for about 20 minutes, or until the bulghar is tender. Check from time to time to see if it has become too dry and add a little more water as necessary.

Meanwhile, heat one-third of the oil in a frying pan over a moderate heat and cook the onion slices with the garlic until brown and just beginning to become caramelized.

Transfer the lentil and bulghar mixture to a warmed serving dish. Dribble over the remaining oil and top with the onion and garlic mixture. Stir the lemon juice into the yogurt and pour it over the middle. Sprinkle the dish with the coriander.

Serve hot, warm or cold, with a green salad.

Top: Chicken and Lamb Couscous (page 47); bottom: Lentil and Bulghar Pilaf with Yogurt

GAME LASAGNE

SERVES 4–6

2 large partridges
400 g/14 oz dessert apples, peeled, cored and thickly sliced
300 ml/½ pt dry cider
300 ml/½ pt game consommé
125 g/4½ oz butter
4 tbsp flour
400 ml/14 fl oz milk
150 ml/¼ pt single cream
225 g/8 oz mature farmhouse Cheddar cheese, grated
1 level tsp ground allspice
1 tbsp oil
400 g/14 oz fresh lasagne, preferably a mixture of colours
30 g/1 oz grated Parmesan cheese
salt and freshly ground black pepper

Preheat the oven to 190C/375F/gas5.

Put the partridges in a baking dish with the apples, cider and consommé. Cover with foil and bake for 20 minutes. Remove from the oven and allow to cool.

When the birds are cool enough to handle, slice the flesh thinly. Using a slotted spoon, transfer the apples to a bowl and reserve the cooking liquid.

Put a large pan of water to heat for the lasagne.

Melt 55 g/2 oz of the butter in a saucepan over moderate heat. Sprinkle in 2 tablespoons of flour and cook for 1 or 2 minutes, stirring continuously. Gradually add the milk to make a smooth liquid. Bring to just below the boil, still stirring continuously, and simmer gently until it thickens. Stir in the cream and cheese and continue to stir until the cheese has all melted. Season.

In another pan make another sauce as above, starting with 55 g/2 oz of the remaining butter and the remaining flour, but adding about 350 ml/12 fl oz of the reserved game cooking liquid instead of milk.

Season with salt, pepper and allspice. Stir in the apples.

When the pasta water is boiling rapidly, add 2 tablespoons of salt and the oil. Drop in the lasagne, bring back to a good rolling boil and cook until just tender but still very firm to the bite. Drain and drop into a pan of cold water.

Grease a large ovenproof casserole with the remaining butter. Spoon some cheese sauce over the bottom and arrange some of the drained lasagne over that. Layer some partridge flesh over the lasagne and spoon some game sauce and apples over that. Continue layering in this way, finishing with some cheese sauce.

Sprinkle with Parmesan and bake for 30 minutes, until bubbling and well browned on top.

TAGLIATELLE WITH ROAST GARLIC

about 30 large garlic cloves, preferably the fresh summer variety, unpeeled
bay leaf
6 tbsp olive oil
55 g/2 oz pine kernels
450 g/1 lb dried tagliatelle
small bunch of basil leaves
1 tbsp balsamic vinegar
salt and freshly ground black pepper
grated Parmesan cheese, to serve

The delicious Italian fresh double-cream cheese MASCARPONE *is now quite widely available over here. More usually served with sugar or fruit at the end of a meal, its subtle flavour and buttery texture are also incomparable in some savoury dishes.*

Preheat the oven to 220C/425F/gas7.

Put the garlic cloves and bay leaf in the centre of a large sheet of foil. Add 2 tablespoons of oil, wrap in a loose parcel and put in a baking dish.

Bake for 20 minutes, or until the garlic is tender but not mushy. About half-way through, add the pine kernels to the oven, scattered on a baking tray.

Meanwhile, put about 4.5 litre/8 pt of water in a pasta pan or large saucepan. Add 2 tablespoons of salt and 1 tablespoon of oil and bring to the boil.

When the water is boiling rapidly, put the pasta in and bring it back to a rolling boil as quickly as possible. Boil rapidly, uncovered, until the pasta is tender but still firm, testing regularly.

Remove the foil parcel and toasted pine kernels from the oven. Take the garlic from the parcel and allow to cool slightly. Squeeze the cloves out of their skins, first snipping off one end if necessary. Keep the pine kernels and garlic cloves warm. Finely chop most of the basil, reserving 12 small leaves.

As soon as the pasta is ready, drain well and stir in the remaining oil, together with most of the garlic and pine kernels, the chopped basil, vinegar and seasonings. Dot the remaining garlic, pine kernels and basil leaves over the top as garnish.

Serve accompanied by grated Parmesan.

PASTA SHELLS WITH MASCARPONE AND NUTS*

170 g/6 oz Mascarpone cheese
30 g/1 oz butter
1 tbsp balsamic vinegar
½ tsp freshly grated nutmeg
450 g/1 lb pasta shells
1 tbsp olive oil
2 egg yolks
(*see page 2 for advice on eggs)
55 g/2 oz Parmesan cheese
85 g/3 oz shelled walnuts, coarsely chopped
salt and freshly ground black pepper

Put the mascarpone in a large serving bowl and stir in the butter, vinegar, a pinch of the nutmeg and seasonings. Place in a warm place in the kitchen.

Cook the pasta in boiling salted and oiled water as described for the tagliatelle. While the pasta is cooking, in another large bowl lightly beat the egg yolks with half the Parmesan and some seasoning.

Drain the pasta quite quickly so that some water still clings to it and immediately stir it well into the egg mixture. The egg should cook on contact.

While the pasta is still very hot, add it to the cheese mixture together with two-thirds of the walnuts and toss to coat uniformly.

Sprinkle over the remaining walnuts, Parmesan and nutmeg to serve.

Clockwise from the top: Tagliatelle with Roast Garlic; Pasta Shells with Mascarpone and Nuts; Spaghettini with Chicken and Aubergine (page 52)

Throughout Italy
many types of
PASTICCIO, or
pasta pies,
are served on
special occasions like
Sunday lunch.
Usually topped with
a pastry lid, they
may be filled with a
wide variety of types
of pasta and other
ingredients,
including
aubergines, Ricotta
cheese and pigeon.

SPAGHETTINI WITH CHICKEN AND AUBERGINE

1 large aubergine, cut into 1 cm/¹/₂ in cubes
6 tbsp olive oil
1 onion, finely chopped
4 garlic cloves, finely chopped
115 g/4 oz chicken breast, cut into 1 cm/¹/₂ in cubes
about 30 stoned black olives
400 g/14 oz canned chopped plum tomatoes
pinch of sugar
1 or 2 tbsp tomato paste
450 g/1 lb dried spaghettini
salt and freshly ground black pepper
chopped basil, parsley or tarragon, to garnish

First make the sauce: sprinkle the aubergine with salt and leave to drain in a colander for about 20 minutes. Rinse well and pat dry.

Heat 2 tablespoons of oil in a sauté pan over a moderate heat and cook the onion for 1 or 2 minutes. Add the garlic and cook for 1 minute more. Using a slotted spoon, transfer the onion and garlic to a bowl.

Add the pieces of chicken to the pan and sauté them briskly for a minute or two, until beginning to brown. Transfer to the bowl.

Add 2 more tablespoons of oil to the pan and sauté the aubergine until gently browned.

Halve some olives for garnish and chop the rest.

Return the chicken, garlic and onion to the pan

along with the chopped olives and the tomatoes with their liquid. Season and add a pinch of sugar. Simmer gently for about 10 minutes. It should be a good thick sauce: adjust the consistency with some tomato paste, as necessary.

Meanwhile, cook the pasta in boiling salted and oiled water until just tender but still firm to the bite, as described for the tagliatelle.

Stir a tablespoon of oil into the cooked and drained pasta and pour the sauce over it. Garnish with the reserved olives and the herbs.

NOTE: add some chopped ham or bacon or a spoonful of brandy when sautéing the chicken for more flavour. This dish is also good for vegetarians without the chicken. Sprinkle with some strips of Mozzarella cheese to make it more substantial.

OPEN PASTICCIO WITH CHICKEN LIVERS

SERVES 6

FOR THE PASTRY
285 g/10 oz flour
140 g/5 oz butter, softened
30 g/1 oz butter
salt and freshly ground black pepper
FOR THE FILLING
450 g/1 lb tagliatelle, preferably a mixture of colours –
white, green, red and black as available
7 tbsp olive oil
1 large onion, finely chopped
3 garlic cloves, finely chopped
85 g/3 oz chicken livers, trimmed
3 tbsp Marsala or sweet sherry
150 ml/¹/₄ pt crème fraîche
115 g/4 oz frozen spinach leaves, defrosted
2 or 3 pinches of freshly ground nutmeg
1 buffalo Mozzarella cheese
2 tbsp finely grated Parmesan cheese

First make the pastry: sift the flour with a pinch of salt and rub the butter into it gently with the fingertips. When it has a crumb-like consistency, add 200 ml/7 fl oz of cold water, a little at a time, to make a smooth dough. Roll into a ball and leave in a cool place for 1 hour.

Roll the rested pastry out to a thickness of about 1 cm/½ in and fold it in three. Roll out and repeat this process twice more and then roll back into a ball and leave to rest for 30 minutes more.

Preheat the oven to 220C/425F/gas7 and generously grease a deep 23 cm/9 in pie dish with butter. Roll out the pastry and use to line the dish.

Make the filling: cook the pasta in boiling salted and oiled water as in the tagliatelle recipe, but stop cooking when just slightly underdone. Drain thoroughly. Stir in 2 tablespoons of oil and season.

While the pasta is cooking, heat 2 tablespoons of the remaining oil in a sauté pan over a moderate heat and sauté the onion for 2 or 3 minutes. Add the garlic and cook for 1 minute more. Then add the chicken livers, and as soon as these change colour, add the Marsala or sherry. Sauté for 1 minute more, stir in the cream and then season. Set aside.

Season the spinach with salt, pepper and nutmeg.

Arrange a layer of half the tagliatelle in the bottom of the pastry case, so that there is a depression in the middle. Pour the chicken liver mixture into the centre. Arrange half the Mozzarella slices on top and then cover these with half the spinach. Put half the remaining tagliatelle on top of this, followed by layers of the remaining Mozzarella, spinach and tagliatelle. Sprinkle over the remaining oil and the Parmesan.

Bake for about 30-35 minutes, until the pastry is firm and the top golden. Leave to cool for 2 or 3 minutes before removing from the pie dish.

Top: Open Pasticcio with Chicken Livers; bottom: Mozzarella and Tomato Salad with Avocado (page 26)

PUDDINGS, CAKES AND SWEETS

*L*ike most Mediterranean food, the desserts of the region reflect the glories of the local produce. With such an abundance of luscious fruits like melons, apricots, citrus fruits, figs and grapes, flavourful nuts such as walnuts, almonds and pistachios, rich aromatic blossom honeys and the wide range of delicious refreshing fresh cheeses and yogurt, there has never really been much place for elaborate creamy gâteaux in the Mediterranean kitchen. Even the pâtisserie of the region makes inspired use of paper-thin filo pastry to produce confections, such as baklava, which are at once richly satisfying but yet lighter and healthier than most of our traditional tarts and pastries.

Top: Yogurt, Date and Honey Cheesecake (page 57);
bottom: Tarte au Citron (page 56)

MARINATED MELON FILLED WITH FRUIT

SERVES 6–8

1 large cantaloupe melon
1 small ripe mango
85 g/3 oz muscat grapes
350 g/12 oz mixed summer fruit, including sweet cherries,
raspberries, strawberries and redcurrants
2 tbsp lemon juice
1 tbsp rose or orange blossom water
2 tbsp Kirsch, Maraschino or Grand Marnier
2-3 tbsp caster sugar
small pinch of salt

Cut a thin slice off the bottom of the melon so that it will sit stably. Cut a 'lid' off the top. Scoop out and discard the seeds. Then scoop out the flesh with a melon baller or spoon, taking care not to pierce the skin.

Peel the mango and chop the flesh into pieces the same size as the pieces of melon. Reserving a few on their stalks for decoration, remove the seeds from the grapes if necessary and halve if large.

Mix the melon flesh with the prepared mango and grapes and half the summer fruit. Mix the lemon juice, rose or orange blossom water and 1 tablespoon of liqueur and stir in all but 1 tablespoon of the sugar and the salt until it has dissolved. Use to dress the fruit, tossing gently to coat well and leave to macerate in the refrigerator for at least 2 hours.

Dissolve the remaining sugar in the remaining liqueur and swirl this mixture around the inside of the melon shell. Put the 'lid' back on the melon shell and leave it to chill with the other fruit.

Just before serving, pile the fruit mixture into the chilled melon shell along with the macerating juices. Arrange the remaining summer fruit so that it spills decoratively from the top.

Melon shells make a delightful way of serving a whole range of dishes in summer. Make ice-cream using the mashed melon flesh mixed with 5 beaten egg yolks and 85 g/3 oz sugar. Beat the mixture over a gentle heat until thick and then fold in 450 ml/¾ pt whipped double cream. Flavour with lemon or lime juice and port, if wished. Freeze, stirring from time to time. Pile into the well-chilled shell, and serve with fruit or raspberry purée.

Alternatively, mix the melon flesh with citrus segments and chopped mint or chunks of avocado, apples and grapes. Dress with a light vinaigrette made with lemon or lime juice and serve in the melon shells as refreshing starters.

T...
n...
BAK...
with...
almo...
and pista...
the pis...
predomina...
nuts may be...
any proportic...
important the...
nuts are not gr...
too finely.

GRANITAS are...
Italian water ices in...
which the formation...
of crystals is...
encouraged to give a...
refreshing grainy...
texture.

t...

Lay...
each...
the o...
Mi...
caster s...

ZABAGLIONE ICE-CREAM*

SERVES 6

12 egg yolks
(*see page 2 for advice on eggs)
115 g/4 oz caster sugar
300 ml/½ pt Marsala
300 ml/½ pt whipping cream
fresh strawberries, raspberries or chopped toasted
hazelnuts, to decorate

In a bowl, beat the egg yolks together with the sugar until pale and thick. Stir in the Marsala and mix well.

Set the bowl over a water bath or on top of a double-boiler and place over a gentle heat. Stir continuously until the custard begins to thicken. Immediately remove from the heat and stand the bottom of the bowl in cold water to stop the cooking, still stirring continuously. Leave aside to cool completely.

Whip the cream until standing in soft peaks and then fold in the egg mixture.

Freeze for about 6 hours in ice trays in the freezer, taking out and stirring vigorously with a fork half-way through to break up the crystals which have formed. Use within 48 hours.

Serve in tall elegant sundae glasses, decorated with fruit or nuts.

NOTE: this makes a very rich ice-cream, but you can lighten it by adding the stiffly beaten whites of 2 or 3 of the eggs to the mixture. The remaining egg whites can be used to make meringues to serve with the ice-cream.

BAKED FIGS STUFFED WITH WALNUTS

12 ripe fresh figs
55 g/2 oz walnut halves
3 tbsp good mild-flavoured honey or soft brown sugar
3 tbsp Madeira or sweet sherry
115 g/4 oz fromage frais

Preheat the oven to 200C/400F/gas6.

Cut a tiny slice off the bottom of each fig so that it will sit stably. Make 2 cuts down through their tops, about 2.5 cm/1 in deep, at right angles to one another. Ease the figs open with a spoon, squeezing their middles at the same time, if necessary.

In a food processor or mortar, grind most of the walnut halves coarsely, reserving the better-looking pieces for decoration. Take care not to over-process.

In a bowl mix the honey or sugar, Madeira or sherry and ground nuts into the fromage frais. Spoon this into the opened-out figs and arrange them in a baking dish.

Bake for about 15-20 minutes, until the cheese is bubbling. Arrange the reserved walnut halves over the tops of the figs to serve.

NOTE: toasted almonds or hazelnuts work equally well in this dish, as does Mascarpone cheese.

ZABAGLIONE is a frothy Italian custard made from egg yolks beaten with sugar and alcohol. Usually served hot in tall glasses, it is most commonly flavoured with Marsala, but some versions use sparkling white wine or even liqueurs.

Baked Figs Stuffed with Walnuts

INDEX

Page numbers in *italic* refer to the photographs

ACKNOWLEDGEMENTS

The Author would like to thank, Marie-Pierre Moine for her advice and encouragement and humbly acknowledges a great debt to the inspirational scholarly work of Claudia Roden and the late Elizabeth David. Also Judith Wills for opening his eyes to the nutritional wisdom of his favourite food.

The Publishers would like to thank the following for the use of accessories in the photography:

Ceramica Blue,
10 Blenheim Crescent,
London W11

The Dining Room Shop
62-64 White Hart Lane,
London SW13

Thomas Goode,
19 South Audley Street,
London W1

Graham & Green,
4 & 7 Elgin Crescent,
London W11

Judy Greenwood Antiques
657 Fulham Road,
London SW6

Homeline Antiques,
33 Parkway,
London NW1